ANDREA JAMES is a Yorta Yorta/Gunaikurnai theatremaker and graduate of VCA. Her plays include *Big Name No Blankets* (co-written with Sammy and Anyupa Butcher), *Yanagai! Yanagai!* (premiered at Playbox in 2004 and toured to the UK), and with Cath Ryan, *Dogged* (Griffin Theatre Company). Her play *Sunshine Super Girl* premiered at Griffith Regional Theatre in 2020, then 2021 Sydney Festival before an extensive national tour. Andrea is currently Associate Artistic Director at Griffin Theatre Company where she directed *Ghosting the Party* by Melissa Bubnic in 2022, *Jailbaby* by Suzie Miller in 2023 and *swim* by Ellen Van Neerven in 2024. Previous positions include Artistic Director of Melbourne Workers Theatre (2001-2008), Aboriginal Arts Development Officer at Blacktown Arts Centre (2010-2012) and Aboriginal Producer at Carriageworks (2012-2016). Andrea was recently awarded the Mona Brand Award for Women Stage and Screen Writers. She was a recipient of British Council's Accelerate Program for Aboriginal Art Leaders and was awarded a Creative Australia National Theatre Award in 2024.

Ian Bliss in rehearsal (Photo: Jacinta Keefe)

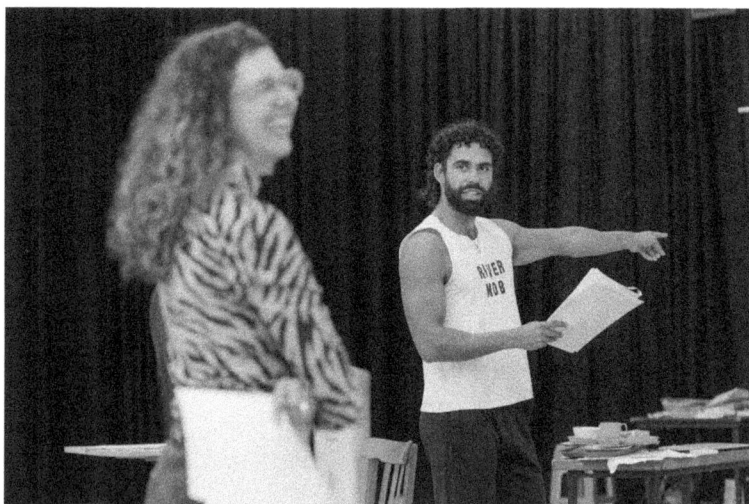

Andrea James and Zach Blampied in rehearsal (Photo: Jacinta Keefe)

THE BLACK WOMAN OF GIPPSLAND

Andrea James

CURRENCY PRESS
The performing arts publisher

**MELBOURNE
THEATRE COMPANY**

CURRENT THEATRE SERIES

First published in 2025
by Currency Press Pty Ltd,
Gadigal Land, Suite 310, 46–56 Kippax Street, Surry Hills, NSW 2010, Australia
enquiries@currency.com.au
www.currency.com.au

in association with Melbourne Theatre Company

Typeset by Brighton Gray for Currency Press.
Cover image shows Chenoa Deemal; photo by Jo Duck.
Cover design by Sarah Ridgway-Cross.

Currency Press acknowledges the Traditional Owners of the Country on which we live and work. We pay our respects to all Aboriginal and Torres Strait Islander Elders, past and present.

Contents

Andrea James in rehearsal (Photo: Jacinta Keefe)

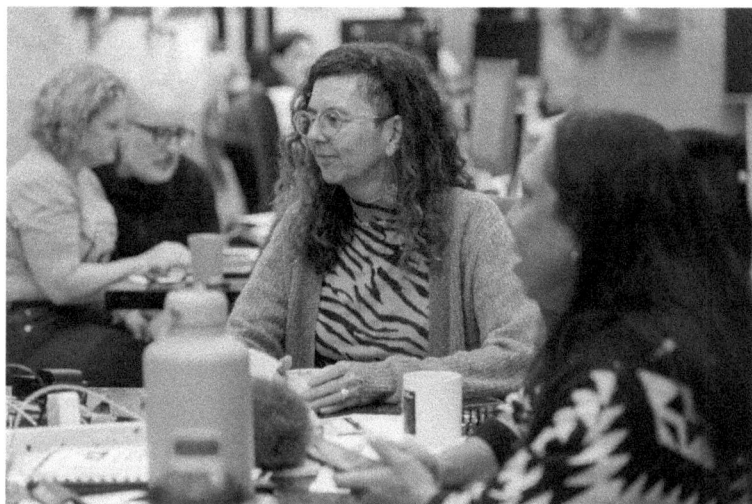

Andrea James in rehearsal (Photo: Jacinta Keefe)

Director's Note

I first heard about the story of The White Woman of Gippsland when I was about ten or eleven years old at my grandmother's house. Our Uncle Phillip Pepper had written a book, *You Are What You Make Yourself to Be,* and it sat proudly on the kitchen table. The most thumbed pages were of the photographs where us descendants of the Peppers would stare into the faces of our forebears—seeing our features mirrored back to us: the cheekbones, the shapes of the eyes and the sadness, at times. Yes, the sadness. I didn't read that book then; rather, I listened to the snippets of stories told by my grandmother and my uncles that bounced around the cups of tea, cigarettes and biscuits.

Later at university as an adolescent (yet to be fully bitten by the theatre bug), I enrolled in a 'First Contact Indigenous Histories' unit and sat in the lecture halls transfixed. The drama of 'first contacts' was rebellious, dangerous, tragic and always electric. It was here that I was once more reunited with this White Woman of Gippsland, who was said to have washed up on a Gunaikurnai beach after a shipwreck. It was as if she was following me around—piquing my curiosity, linking me with my grandmother's country and setting me on a path that I would later tread.

When I was offered a Melbourne Theatre Company commission under the NEXT STAGE program, The White Woman of Gippsland immediately came to mind. Not just because I wanted to debunk a deathly myth, but to hold Melbourne (on Kulin Nations Country) to account. It is here, at the exclusive Melbourne Club in the 1840s, that the idea to form and fund (not one, but two) expedition parties, to rescue a 'damsel in distress' was launched. The consequences were disastrous for the Gunaikurnai and would lead to dispossession of land and murder on a tragic scale. We fought back courageously. We still do.

From the outset, I knew I wanted to ground this story in the now, to disempower urban and colonial myths that continue to have repercussions for First Nations people right around Australia.

For two years, I literally wrestled with the archival material surrounding this 'event'. The act of writing is a powerful force that lays down a kind of truth that can sometimes stand in counterpoint to yarning oral history. Writing can hold stories hostage; it traps them and assumes the truth. It stands over the hum and vibration, magic and power of the spoken word. It is a tension that rubs and has led to extraordinary advances by Indigenous Thinkers ('Blakademics') that have expanded academic disciplines for the better.

Walking on country has been a vital part of the rehearsal process. Connecting with our elders—Aunty Glenys Watts, Aunty Doris Paton and Uncle Wayne Thorpe—has been a vital bridge back to the five clans of the Gunaikurnai. Their support and encouragement have meant the world to me and the team.

It has been deeply satisfying to release the language words that Alfred Howitt published in 1904, which captured remnants of Gunaikurnai songs about the observations of a shipwreck and the caring of a white woman. Through deeply embedded cultural knowledge, Gunnai Lore man Uncle Wayne Thorpe has translated and re-arranged the songs and sung them back into being.

Ultimately, it is country that informs us. It is country that we read like a book. It is country that gives us the first word and always has the last.

Thank you to our allies: Jen Medway, Melbourne Theatre Company Head of New Work and, as it turns out, a bloody good bus driver who, amongst other things, supported our cultural groundwork on country; to Patricia Cornelius, my 'Theatre Mum' and long-term champion who I can always rely upon to tell it like it is; and the countless colleagues and 'Blakademics' who provided a third eye to the script and prompted me to dig deeper.

Finally, to my cousin, Brent Watkins—mover and shaker—whose cultural integrity and commitment has etched a cultural mark on this production that runs deep and provides connection and healing.

Andrea James

The Black Woman of Gippsland was first performed by Melbourne Theatre Company at Southbank Theatre, The Sumner, Melbourne, on the lands of the Boon Wurrung and Wurundjeri Woi Wurrung peoples of the Kulin Nation, on 5 May 2025, with the following cast and creatives:

KYLE/WILLAMBULUNG/ENSEMBLE	Zach Blampied
JACINTA/ENSEMBLE	Chenoa Deemal
DANCER/PERFORMER	Brent Watkins
AUNTY ROCHELLE/ENSEMBLE	Ursula Yovich
SERGEANT/ENSEMBLE	Ian Bliss

Writer/Director, Andrea James
Choreographer, Brent Watkins
Gunnai Cultural Consultant for the Gunaikurnai, Wayne Thorpe
Set & Costume Designer, Romanie Harper
Lighting Designer, Verity Hampson
Composer & Sound Designer, James Henry
AV Designer, Rhian Hinkley
Associate Director, Amy Sole
Dramaturg, Patricia Cornelius
Dramaturg, Jennifer Medway
Stage Manager, Jess Keepence
Assistant Stage Manager, Lucie Sutherland
Stage Management Secondment (VCA), Alicia Guiney

Presented in association with
YIRRAMBOI
NEXTSTAGE
Commissioned and developed through Melbourne Theatre Company's NEXT STAGE Writers' Program, with the support of our Playwrights Giving Circle.

Brent Watkins and Zach Blampied in rehearsal (Photo: Jacinta Keefe)

Chenoa Deemal and Brent Watkins in rehearsal (Photo: Jacinta Keefe)

Melbourne Theatre Company acknowledges the Boon Wurrung and Wurundjeri Woi Wurrung peoples of the Kulin Nation, the Traditional Custodians of the land on which we work, create and gather. We pay our respects to all First Nations people, their Elders past and present, and their enduring connections to Country, knowledge, and stories. As a Company we remain committed to the invitation of the Uluru Statement from the Heart and its call for voice, truth and treaty.

Chenoa Deemal in rehearsal (Photo: Jacinta Keefe)

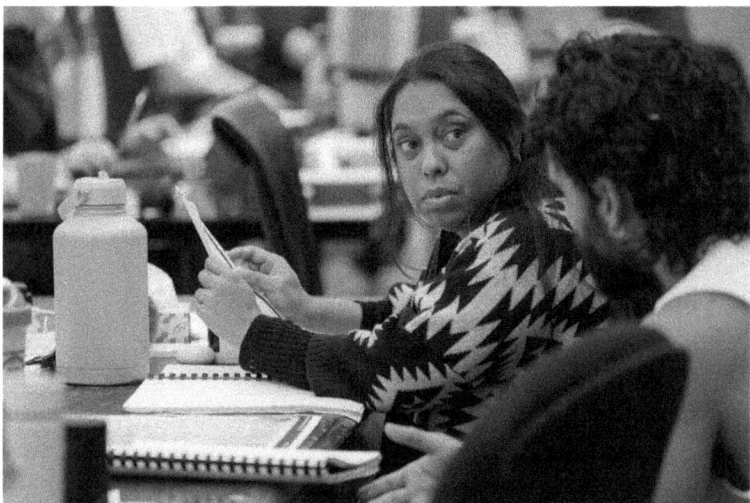

Chenoa Deemal in rehearsal (Photo: Jacinta Keefe)

Ursula Yovich and Ian Bliss in rehearsal (Photo by Jacinta Keefe)

Ursula Yovich and Ian Bliss in rehearsal (Photo by Jacinta Keefe)

'The world I inhabit has been created by ancestral creator beings and it is organic and alive with spirits and signs which inform my way of knowing. Thus respect and caution frame my approach to knowledge production; the more that I know the less that I know because there are other forms of knowledge that exist beyond us as humans.'

Doctor. Aileen Moreton-Robinson

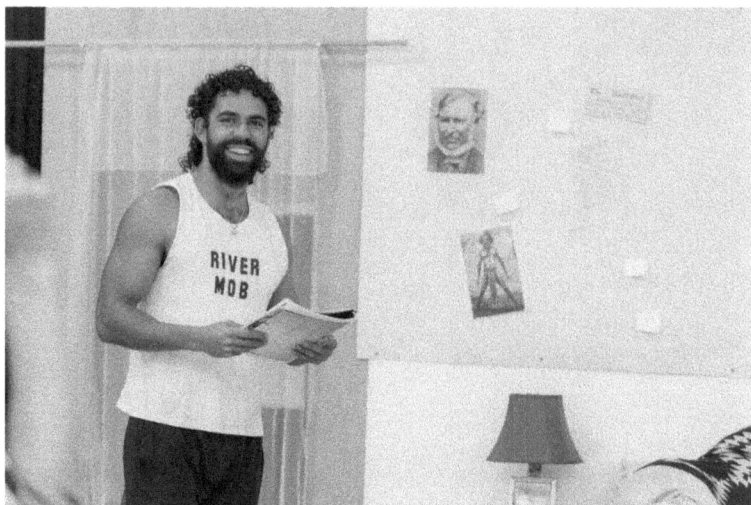

Zach Blampied in rehearsal (Photo by Jacinta Keefe)

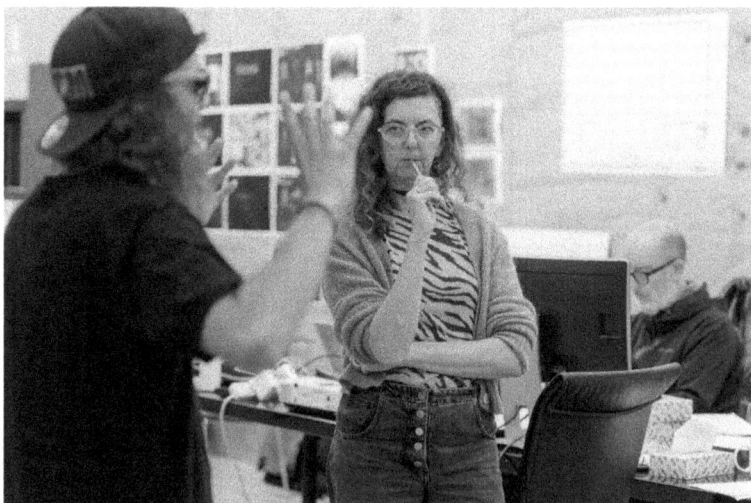

Andrea James and Brent Watkins in rehearsal (Photo by Jacinta Keefe)

Acknowledgements

Doctor. Lou Bennett
Doctor. Julia Hurst
Doctor. Shino Konishi
Doctor. Romaine Moreton
Ms. Kimberley Moulton
Doctor. Doris Paton
Doctor. Liza-Mare Syron
Aunty Glenys Watts

Gunaikurnai songs translated and arranged by Wayne Thorpe
of the Gunnai people, and used with permission

The late Aunty Oodgeroo Noonuccal excerpt from poem
'A Song of Hope' used with permission

Thank You

Bryan Andy
Kamarra Bell-Wykes
Patricia Cornelius (Dramaturg)
Float Studio
Declan Greene
Rob Hudson
Peter Matheson
Chris Mead
Jen Medway (Dramaturg)
Francesca Smith
Wayne Thorpe

Development Actors

Zac Blampied
Sid Brisbane
NazAree Dickerson
Phoebe Grainer
Monica Karo
Ari Maza-Long
Tully Narkle
Melodie Reynolds Djarra

CHARACTERS

JACINTA* (also plays BLACKFELLA 1)

AUNTY ROCHELLE* (also plays HOTEL MANAGER, WHITE WOMAN, BLACKFELLA 2, TROOPER)

KYLE*, Jacinta's cousin brother (also plays WILLAMBULUNG, BLACKFELLA 3, TROOPER)

DANCER*, a shapeshifting non-speaking role that facilitates Blackfella ceremony and spirit. He is the past and the present (also plays BUNGELENE and WHITE WOMAN when required).

SERGEANT (also plays SUPERVISOR, DE VILLIERS, TROOPER, GHOSTS).

* Must be performed by Aboriginal actors.

SETTING

A cop shop. An academic's office. A caravan. A typical motel room in rural Australia with all the usual trappings. The room is on Gunaikurnai Country and has a wondrous capacity to shapeshift and dissolve to allow the natural world to reclaim it.

Time and place—as well as the dead and the living—are porous.

ORDER OF SCENES AND TIMELINE

Prologue: Maybe
Dreaming—No time in particular.

Scene 1: Motel & Cop Shop
Present—Phone call, five days after Jacinta went missing.
Hotel Room—The day Jacinta arrived at the motel.

Scene 2: The Little Caravan
Present—One week before Jacinta goes missing.
Two weeks before proposal is due.

Scene 3: Supervision
Present—Same day, one week before Jacinta goes missing.
Two weeks before the proposal is due.

Scene 4: Kyle's Dribble
Present—One day before Jacinta goes missing.
One week before proposal is due.

Scene 5: Motel & Cop Shop Thriller
Present—Five days after Jacinta went missing.
One week before proposal is due.

Scene 6: Motel Room—I Saw Her
Present—Into the night and next day, six days after Jacinta
went missing.
Six days before proposal is due.

Scene 7: More Supervision
Present—Two days before proposal is due.

Scene 8: Motel Room—History Repeating
Present—One day before the proposal is due.

Scene 9: More Cop Shop
Present—Seven days after Jacinta went missing.

Scene 10: Remembering
Present—Motel room, the night before the proposal is due.

Scene 11: Cop Shop Again
Present—Same day, seven days after Jacinta went missing.

Scene 12: Procrastination Blues
Present—Motel room, the night before the proposal is due.

Scene 13: Empty Caravan
Present—Seven days after Jacinta went missing.

Scene 14: Motel Dreaming
Present/Past merging—Deep dark night, the night before the
proposal is due.

This playtext went to press before the end of rehearsals and may differ from the play as performed.

PROLOGUE—MAYBE

The DANCER *sings and/or dances the traditional Gunaikurnai song of shipwreck.*

DANCER: **Blaung-a-wrekwa tauraua koolin-guka**
(*ropes-tail of the tall mast, Burning white-fellows*)
wuroong toonkoo bata-tunga
(*flame boughs mast and down*)
budda-ngaioo Tuka-bunda Kunnun-guka,
(*me and White-woman-hit, make this blackfulla-feel no good,*)
ma-Kunnung-ita
(*I leave it there.*)

BLACKFELLAS 1, 2 *and* 3 *arrive and stand on a wild and rugged beach.*

BLACKFELLA 1: At first we thought it could be a baby whale.
Washed up.
Or a massive seal.

BLACKFELLA 3: We see this lump

BLACKFELLA 2: This sodden lump, laying there in the sand.

BLACKFELLA 1: And as we get closer we see a pile of clothes and rags and hair and arms

BLACKFELLA 2: Fluorescent legs,

BLACKFELLA 1: Face-down,
Sand and weed stuck to her face.
Lips blue.

BLACKFELLA 3: There she lay.
Bedraggled, sad,

BLACKFELLA 1: She fascinates us.

BLACKFELLA 3: That one boot missing and a stocking torn.

BLACKFELLA 2: We thought it was her skin.
All frills and coats

BLACKFELLA 1: The deathly dampness of her skirts that pulled her down.
Orange hair spread out like tentacles.

BLACKFELLA 3: The men poke at her with the kind end of their spears

BLACKFELLA 1: Her eyes flash terror
       Then she closes them again.
BLACKFELLA 2: Sleeping
BLACKFELLA 3: Or dying
BLACKFELLA 1: Or drowning
BLACKFELLA 2: Or all of the above.
BLACKFELLA 1: The wave put her there.
BLACKFELLA 2: She rolls over onto her back
BLACKFELLA 1: The lumps under her clothes tell us she is woman.
BLACKFELLA 3: Chest rises and falls
BLACKFELLA 2: She coughs and water comes out.
BLACKFELLA 3: Foam and phlegm.
BLACKFELLA 1: She stands up
BLACKFELLA 3: She falls.
BLACKFELLA 2: Makes sounds and falls.
BLACKFELLA 1: Desperate for water we lead her to the creek.
       She drinks and vomits and drinks again.
BLACKFELLA 2: We feed her up.
       And she eats.
       She sits by the fire and the women touch her hair
       The hem of her dress.
       Her toes.
       That one boot missing and we tap it as if to ask
       Where's the other one?
BLACKFELLA 1: She nods and waves her arms in the air.
       Points to the sea.
       But we already know that's where she's come from.
BLACKFELLA 2: Where's your children? Your man?
       We tap her stomach and point to a man.
BLACKFELLA 1: Stinging scratchy itchy.
       Her dress sticks to her arms.
BLACKFELLA 3: Won't let go.
BLACKFELLA 2: Aunty puts a possum-skin cloak around her
       She lays down and shivers and sleeps.
BLACKFELLA 3: And the children stare.
       Eyes wide.

BLACKFELLA 2: And the stories begin of how and why she's come to
    our camp.
    Will we take her with us?
    Or leave her there?
BLACKFELLA 1: Next day we pack our things.
    Walk away.
    She grabs her dress
    Possum-skin cloak
BLACKFELLA 3: She follows us.
BLACKFELLA 2: Like we her family.
BLACKFELLA 1: Sleeps and eats and follows for days.
BLACKFELLA 2: Weeks
BLACKFELLA 3: Months
BLACKFELLA 1: Years
BLACKFELLA 2: And Aunty makes her a daughter.
BLACKFELLA 1: And Uncle makes her his wife.
BLACKFELLA 2: Kin way, if she's going to stay.
BLACKFELLA 1: Maybe we took you by the hand,
    Oh White Woman of Gippsland …
BLACKFELLA 2: Maybe we saved you …
BLACKFELLA 3: Maybe, you were never there …
BLACKFELLA 1: But, whatever, you changed our lives.
ALL: Forever.

SCENE 1—MOTEL AND COP SHOP

Darkness. A telephone rings.

*Lights up on a dimly lit and aged motel room. Curtains struggle to keep
out the light and heat of the outside. The shadow of a cleaner wheeling
her trolley throws up on the curtains. There is a sliding window/hatch
that delivers breakfasts onto a bench.*

We hear a conversation as a voiceover.

SERGEANT: Hello, Sale Police Station.
ROCHELLE: I'd like to report a missing woman.
SERGEANT: I see. When did you last see her?
ROCHELLE: Five days ago.

SERGEANT: Name?

ROCHELLE: Please, can you find her?

SERGEANT: We need some details first.

ROCHELLE: She never goes away this long.

SERGEANT: I need a name.

ROCHELLE: Jacinta. Pepper.

Beat.

JACINTA *enters the motel room, slams the door and leans against it. Agitated.*

SERGEANT: Pepper. What's your relationship to this person?

ROCHELLE: I'm her aunt. Please, can you get a car out to look for her?

SERGEANT: Where are her parents?

ROCHELLE: Deceased. I've been Jacinta's mother since …

SERGEANT: How old is Jacinta?

ROCHELLE: Twenty-six. Born on the first of May 1998.

SERGEANT: Nationality?

ROCHELLE: Yorta Yorta and Gunaikurnai.

JACINTA *steps into the room and stands. Fixed.*

SERGEANT: Aboriginal.

Beat.

Does she have a history of running away?

ROCHELLE: She's a grown woman.

Beat.

SERGEANT: Pepper?

JACINTA *sits on the motel room bed.*

A lovers' spat perhaps?

ROCHELLE: What?

SERGEANT: Did she have a fight with her boyfriend?

ROCHELLE: She doesn't have a boyfriend.

SERGEANT: Girlfriend?

JACINTA *gets up and paces.*

ROCHELLE: No.

SERGEANT: Does she live alone?

ROCHELLE: She lives with us.

SERGEANT: Children?

ROCHELLE: No.

SERGEANT: Does she have a history of drug use?

ROCHELLE: No.

SERGEANT: Alcohol dependence?

ROCHELLE: No!

SERGEANT: Unemployment? Sickness benefits?

> JACINTA *walks to the window, looks out the curtains and sits on the bed again.*

ROCHELLE: No. She's at university.

SERGEANT: University?

> *Beat.*

> And when did you say you last saw her?

ROCHELLE: Five days ago. Sometimes she goes away for a weekend to clear her head. Takes her tent with her, but she always comes back after a day or two. Please, can you get a car out now?

SERGEANT: Has she been in contact with any other members of the family?

ROCHELLE: Not her brother, her cousins, her friends. No-one.

SERGEANT: You'll have to come into the station.

> Bring a photo. A current one.

> *The phone hangs up.*

> JACINTA *stands. Breathes in. Breathes out.*

SCENE 2—THE LITTLE CARAVAN

JACINTA *is in her caravan. A cheap and slow laptop throws a dull blue light onto* JACINTA*'s face. She squints into the screen. She types a sentence. Reads it. Deletes it. Tries again. Reads it. Slams the laptop shut.*

There's a sharp knock on the door. KYLE *enters.*

JACINTA: I didn't say 'come in'.
KYLE: Yeah, but I knocked.
JACINTA: Yeah, but I didn't say you could come in.
KYLE: Yeah, but I knocked.

> KYLE *sits at the table and flicks through some of the papers.*

Whatcha doin'?
JACINTA: Nothin'.
KYLE: Doesn't look like nothin'. Can I borrow twenty bucks?
JACINTA: I gave you twenty yesterday.
KYLE: Spent it.

> KYLE *grabs a rubber stress ball off* JACINTA*'s table and handballs it against the wall.*

JACINTA: Why aren't you at school?
KYLE: Don't tell Mum.
JACINTA: Bloody hell, Kyle! You're gonna get me in trouble again.
KYLE: I hate that place.
JACINTA: You've gotta get ready for your Year Twelve.
KYLE: No way! That's two years away!

> KYLE *looks around the van.*

Gee, sis, you've let yourself go. This place is a mess.
Do you ever let yourself outta here?

> *He finally sits and flicks through the bills on* JACINTA*'s fridge.*

What's all these bills?
JACINTA: Stop sticky-beaking!

> *She grabs the bills off him.*

What electives did you choose this year?

KYLE: I dunno. What for?

JACINTA: Think about the sort of job you want.

KYLE: There's no jobs.

JACINTA: There's plenty of jobs.

KYLE: Not for people like us.

JACINTA: Come on, mate, you only get one chance at school.

KYLE: Why is it so boring then?

JACINTA: They're gonna throw you out!

KYLE: Good.

JACINTA: Not good.

> *She flips up her laptop again.*

KYLE: Can I have twenty bucks? I'm meeting the boys down at the shops.

JACINTA: Your mum doesn't want you hanging around with those boys. And will you stop bouncing that bloody ball?!

KYLE: Is this stress ball stressing you out? It shouldn't. It's a stress ball. It's supposed to alleviate stress.

> KYLE *squeezes the ball in front of* JACINTA*'s face.*

See?

JACINTA: YOU stress me out!

> JACINTA *grabs the ball off* KYLE.

I've got two weeks to hand this paper in. Now get out.

KYLE: Give me twenty bucks then I'll go.

JACINTA: Shop's shut. The Bank of Jacinta is officially closed.

KYLE: Come yabbying then.

JACINTA: No.

KYLE: I'm going to that dam your mum used to take us.

She pulled those yabbies in five or six on the same line. 'Til that farmer came up to tell us we were trespassing.

Jarred him right up. Told him it was our land and that we had hunting rights.

> JACINTA *is unmoved.*

Come on …

JACINTA: I've got a deadline.

KYLE: You're boring.

KYLE *flicks through some more of the paperwork.*

What is this stuff?

JACINTA: Squatters' diaries.

KYLE: McMillan, McAlister, King, Anderson. I know those names.

JACINTA: The squattocracy. Land-grabbers.

KYLE: Thirteenth July 1843, two hundred and forty-nine sheep.

Twentieth July 1843, two hundred and twelve sheep.

Twenty-third July 1843, two hundred and six sheep.

These fellas just counting sheep!

JACINTA: Yeah, but that's not all they're counting.

See here?

Where they all go to the waterhole on the same day?

KYLE: Yeah.

JACINTA: What do you think those fullas were doing?

See this map here. Butchers Creek. Slaughterhouse Gully. Skull Creek. These fullas weren't washing sheep.

Beat.

KYLE: Shit. That's full-on.

JACINTA: Yep. Sometimes you've gotta read between the lines.

KYLE: How many words do you have to write?

JACINTA: Too many.

KYLE: How many?

JACINTA: About eight thousand.

She takes the paperwork off KYLE. *He finds something else to fidget with.*

KYLE: Fuck. That's a lot of words.

JACINTA: Yep, it's for my confirmation paper and then, if they let me, I'll write eighty thousand words.

KYLE: Shit. That's hardcore. Studying is for nerds.

JACINTA: I'm not a nerd. I'm a 'blakademic'.

KYLE: What you want to be a bigshot for anyway? You already got one degree!

JACINTA: Gotta find a good research question first.

KYLE: I've got a good question.

JACINTA: What?

KYLE: Can I have twenty bucks?

JACINTA: No.

KYLE: Please. I'll pay ya back.

JACINTA: No.

KYLE: What ya gonna do with all those words?

JACINTA: I'm gonna save the world.

> KYLE *and* JACINTA *do a high five.*

Now, get out.

> AUNTY ROCHELLE *knocks on the door.*

ROCHELLE: Are you in?

> KYLE *gesticulates wildly as he mouths silently to* JACINTA.

KYLE: Tell her you're busy!

JACINTA: [*mouthing back*] What?

ROCHELLE: Jacinta, are you there?

JACINTA: Hang on …

ROCHELLE: There's a phone call for you in the house.

> KYLE *is begging* JACINTA.

JACINTA: Come in …

KYLE: [*still mouthing silently*] Fuck.

> ROCHELLE *enters.* KYLE *tries to hide.*

ROCHELLE: Kyle! You were meant to be at school two hours ago.

KYLE: It's just that stupid Pathways class. It's bullshit. Tell them I'm sick.

ROCHELLE: I'm not telling them you're sick. You. Get to school!

KYLE: I don't wanna go.

JACINTA: Do what your mum says.

KYLE: No.

> KYLE *goes to leave.* ROCHELLE *grabs him by the shoulder and sits him down.*

ROCHELLE: You. Stay there.

KYLE: This is bullshit.

ROCHELLE: [*to* JACINTA] What's wrong with your mobile phone?

JACINTA: I turned it off! I'm busy!

ROCHELLE: There's a phone call in the house. Some fulla. Says he's your supervisor.

KYLE: You're under supervision?

JACINTA: Shit!

ROCHELLE: [*to* KYLE] You. Shut up.

KYLE: Sounds like jail!

> ROCHELLE *glares at* KYLE.

JACINTA: It is.

> KYLE *tries to sneak out of the van.* AUNTY ROCHELLE *pushes him back onto the seat.*

ROCHELLE: You're going to school. And what's wrong with you? You haven't been yourself lately.

JACINTA: I have to finish this paper.

ROCHELLE: You haven't slept for days. I can see your light on from the house. You're up all night!

JACINTA: I've just gotta get this done.

ROCHELLE: But is it making you happy?

JACINTA: [*grumpily*] I *AM* happy!

ROCHELLE: You should go out more. Spend some time with your friends.

JACINTA: Mum would want me to do this.

> AUNTY ROCHELLE *looks inside* JACINTA*'s cupboards.*

ROCHELLE: And you've gotta eat more.

JACINTA: What are you? The welfare?

ROCHELLE: I'm worried about you, that's all.

> JACINTA *flips her laptop open again.*

JACINTA: Did Uncle Phillip ever tell you about that White Woman of Gippsland?

ROCHELLE: Yeah, he used to tell us that story all the time.

JACINTA: Why did they call her Lohan (*'loo-an'*) Tuka (*'tucker'*)?

> KYLE *tries to sneak out again.*

> ROCHELLE *gives him side-eye and he sits down again.*

ROCHELLE: 'Lohan'. That's our language word for 'stranger' or 'not from here' …

JACINTA: … and 'Tuka' means wife …

ROCHELLE: Woman. 'The gatherer of tucker.'

JACINTA: Stranger woman.

ROCHELLE: They reckon she had long red hair down to her moom and that she lived in a cave.

KYLE: I know that cave! It's haunted as.

ROCHELLE: You're not allowed to go down there.

KYLE: Some of the fellas go down there to have bongs.

ROCHELLE *glares at him.*

Not me! I don't go down there.

JACINTA: Where's this cave?

ROCHELLE: You should talk to Aunty Ginny. There's an old-language song. Something about giving this white woman from a big canoe a possum-skin cloak. All in language. Her mother used to sing it to us sometimes when we were being naughty. Scared the shit out of me. I can't remember how it went, but Aunty would remember.

JACINTA: I'll drop in there tomorrow.

ROCHELLE: She's got heaps of yarns. Shit! I'm late for work.

ROCHELLE *grabs* KYLE *by the arm.*

ROCHELLE: I'm dropping you off to school.

KYLE: I don't want to.

They go to exit.

ROCHELLE: Shit! That fulla's still on the phone! What do you want me to tell him?

JACINTA: Tell him my dog ate my homework.

ROCHELLE: Can you drop Kyle off to the finals tomorrow? I don't want him wandering the streets.

They go to exit.

ROCHELLE: What do you want me to tell him!

JACINTA: Who?

ROCHELLE: This fulla on the phone.

JACINTA: Tell him I'm coming in. Shit!

ROCHELLE *exits.*

KYLE: You know, if I've got a problem, I just go down to the river and sit on a rock.

JACINTA *looks at him quizzically.*

ROCHELLE: [*offstage*] Kyle!!

He exits.

The DANCER *sings and/or dances the traditional Gunaikurnai song of the White Woman.*

DANCER: **Yoowa-tha, kaiyun,**
(*Give, possum-string skirt,*)
loohan-tuka, moku-katung
(*white-woman, from overseas*)
Narrau-ungal
(*Blanket*)
muntoo wanga-na
(*there locational—from*
wanga = with, na = having, excluding others
'put the blanket there with her')

SCENE 3—SUPERVISION

JACINTA *sits opposite her* SUPERVISOR.

JACINTA: There's something troubling me about this White Woman of Gippsland story.

SUPERVISOR: You and a hundred other historians. There's a lot of writing on this subject. Come on, I'm on your team. If you're going to try and pursue this, you have to find a whole new area of research.

JACINTA: I've just got a feeling …

SUPERVISOR: You can't submit a thesis based on a hunch. You need a strong foundation of primary material to support your argument. Assemble the facts. Why don't you reference Spencer?

JACINTA: Your mate?

SUPERVISOR: My colleague. He's the pre-eminent scholar in this field and an expert on Angus McMillan. I know you've read his work.

Get back to the diaries of McLeod who was in the second expedition party. His records were sporadic, but informative nonetheless.

JACINTA: Everything is so contradictory.

SUPERVISOR: My methodology book is just about to go to print, but you're welcome to read an advanced copy if you like?

JACINTA: Oh. Okay.

SUPERVISOR: You can review it and quote from it. It could be good for your dissertation.

JACINTA: Ah, right. Thanks.

SUPERVISOR: Come on, you're nearly there. I recommend you read John Adams' *Notes on Gippsland History*, volumes one to four, Jessie Harrison's *Memories of Old Gippsland and its Earliest Pioneers* and Don Watson's *Caledonia Australis: Scottish highlanders on the frontier of Australia*.

JACINTA: I've read them.

SUPERVISOR: Then read them again.

JACINTA: It feels like something is missing.

SUPERVISOR: Keep digging.

JACINTA: I want to know more about Indigenous Ways of Knowing. How many academics are writing from a Gunaikurnai perspective?

SUPERVISOR: Exactly. We want you to do well. So keep going. What is your evidence?

JACINTA: I'll use oral history.

SUPERVISOR: Good. But you'll have to get approval from the Ethics Committee to formalise your interviews.

JACINTA: This is how it works. I bump into someone in the supermarket who tells me her aunty heard something about this story from her grandmother. Aunty tells me the story and then says 'Go see old uncle down the road.' You walk down to Uncle's place, but he's away at a funeral. Then I go back to Aunty again and her daughter tells me she's gone on a cruise to Thailand (even though she gets seasick). Then Uncle comes back from sorry business and wants me to take him to the supermarket and *then* he'll have a yarn. I can't pre-empt or plan for that. This is oral history. You have to have lots of cups of tea. Yarning.

SUPERVISOR: You have to have ethics approval to protect vulnerable communities.

JACINTA: I'm related to them. They're family.

SUPERVISOR: I understand that, but ethics approval is an important part of the academic process.

JACINTA: That will take months. These timelines don't take into account sorry business, low literacy rates, closing the gap. I have to record these stories now before it's too late.

SUPERVISOR: You can't retrospectively include any interviews before Ethics Committee approval.

JACINTA: Yarns. Yarns are hearing stories whenever and however they arise before they disappear. And you've gotta wait. Elders don't give you a story until you're ready.

SUPERVISOR: You've gone through four supervisors. In fact, there are no more supervisors in this department who can oversee your work. I'm it! I'm here to help you.

Pause.

Are you sure this is what you want to do?

JACINTA: Yes. I have to.

SCENE 4—KYLE'S DRIBBLE

The DANCER *and* KYLE *play one on one basketball together. It could be a game, or it could be a dance. Or both.*

Lights cross to JACINTA *typing on her laptop. On a roll. In the zone.*

ROCHELLE *knocks on the caravan door and enters.*

ROCHELLE: Where the fuck is Kyle?

JACINTA: I dunno.

ROCHELLE: You were supposed to pick him up after the game!

JACINTA: Shit! I'm sorry, I completely forgot.

ROCHELLE: I don't want Kyle walking around this town at night.

JACINTA: I'm sorry, I got distracted …

ROCHELLE: I missed his final so I could work a shift and I just asked you to do one thing …

JACINTA: I'm sorry.

ROCHELLE: I don't want this kid walking around at night.

JACINTA: I'm sorry. I've been really busy, I got distracted.

ROCHELLE: Too busy for family?

JACINTA: That's not what I said …

KYLE *enters without knocking. He wears a medal for player of the match.*

KYLE: Kyle Pepper intercepts the ball, drives it up the lane with a fast break, sidesteps two freckly giants, v-cuts, dribbles, three steps, runs, dribbles. Sets it up with a behind the back pass, loads the gun and … SCORES!

Ahhhhhhhh!

He makes a crowd noise.

The crowd goes wild. Kyle Pepper just dropped a three-pointer for the win for the District Under-Sixteens' Basketball Championship! And we're on our way to the State League.

I got player of the match. Doosh!

You shoulda been there.

He slam dunks and shoots imaginary basketballs.

Check out my medal!

He gammin spits and polishes it.

I reckon there were some selectors in the crowd tonight. I'm gonna get picked for the Lakers and move us all to LA. Yep. And I'll set youse all up in my penthouse. I'll have so much cash I won't know what to do with it. I'll have those big chunky gold chains and Mum, you can have all the shoes you want and, Jacinta, you won't have to study anymore. I will provide.

Pause.

What's wrong with you two?

JACINTA/ROCHELLE: Nothing.

Silence.

ROCHELLE: [*to* JACINTA] I asked you to do one thing.

JACINTA: I'm sorry.

ROCHELLE: To pick him up.

JACINTA: I told you, I'm sorry.

KYLE: I'm alright. / I got home okay.

ROCHELLE: And maybe you can help out around the yard sometimes?

JACINTA: Alright. I will.

ROCHELLE: Those weeds don't pull themselves up on their own, you know.

JACINTA: Okay, okay.

ROCHELLE: Just sweep up now and then …

JACINTA: Okay.

ROCHELLE: Or bring the washing in.

JACINTA: Alright!

ROCHELLE: And it wouldn't hurt to come in and say hi, now and then.

JACINTA: I've got one week to get this research proposal in.

ROCHELLE: Doesn't mean you can't put in around the house a bit more.

JACINTA: I am putting in! Every day. Trying to make this fucking degree count.

ROCHELLE: While everything around you is falling to pieces. And don't swear.

JACINTA: Stop acting like you're my mum!

ROCHELLE: I'm not your mum!

JACINTA: No, you're not.

ROCHELLE: I can never be your mum …

JACINTA: That's right! So leave me alone!

JACINTA *grabs her backpack, books and laptop.*

ROCHELLE: Hey! Where you going?

JACINTA: Out!

JACINTA *exits.*

ROCHELLE: Shit!

You should've called her to come pick you up.

What's wrong with your bloody phone?

KYLE: Got no credit.

ROCHELLE: Again!?

KYLE *bounces and shoots another imaginary goal.*

KYLE: Doosh! Three points!

SCENE 5—MOTEL AND COP SHOP THRILLER

At the motel, JACINTA *places a framed photo and a candle on the bedside table as a makeshift shrine to her mother.*

Crossfade to the cop shop.

ROCHELLE: I've been up and down the country for days. From Lakes Entrance to Warragul. All her favourite camping spots, dropped into her cousin's place at Morwell, our Aunty's here at Sale. I've put it out on the Black grapevine everywhere and nobody has seen or heard a thing. I even went to the cemetery where her mum's buried.

Silence.

To see if she put flowers there.

Beat.

SERGEANT: When did you last have contact with her?

ROCHELLE: She was in the caravan out the back. She was coming and going a lot. And when she was home she'd keep to herself. She had a deadline.

SERGEANT: Deadline?

ROCHELLE: She's doing her PhD.

SERGEANT: She must be a pretty smart cookie then?

ROCHELLE: Yes. She's smart alright. Like her mother.

Pause.

She's been missing for five days! What if someone's got her?

SERGEANT: Nine times out of ten, a missing person doesn't want to be found …

Cross to motel room.

JACINTA *lights the candle, takes a painting off the wall and paces. She grabs a fat texta and shakes it.*

Cross to cop shop.

ROCHELLE: She hasn't posted on Facebook, texted or called for days. Her bank account was emptied on the day she went missing.

SERGEANT: She might just need a break. You haven't seen her for five days and you knew she was under a lot of pressure?

ROCHELLE: She had a deadline.

SERGEANT: Have you called her?

ROCHELLE: Of course!

SERGEANT: And she's not picking up?

ROCHELLE: No.

SERGEANT: Maybe she's avoiding you?

ROCHELLE: She wouldn't do that.

SERGEANT: Would you consider Jacinta a happy person?

ROCHELLE: Once. She used to be a really happy kid.

Pause.

Jacinta and I had a stupid argument.

SERGEANT: An argument? Was there violence?

ROCHELLE: No! We argue sometimes but she always comes back.

Beat.

What if she's hurt herself?

SERGEANT: She's harmed herself before?

ROCHELLE: No. I'm just worried she might.

Cross back to motel room.

JACINTA *grabs a fat texta and shakes it.*

She draws a giant tribal map onto the wall and pays her respects.

She writes the names onto the wall.

JACINTA: Brataualung (*bra-toor-a-loong*)
Tatungalung (*ta-tung-a-loong*)
Brayakaulung (*bra-yuka-loong*)
Brabralung (*bra-beera-loong*)
Krautungalung (*krow-a-tung-a-loong*)

JACINTA *sniffs the texta and talks to the photo of her mum.*

It's alright, Mum. It's not permanent. Promise –

She scrawls the numbers '1839' onto the wall.

November 1839. The ship *Britannia*, en route to Sydney shipwrecks ... here. Just off Brataualung Country.

She draws a ship on the wall and scrawls the words 'Britannia' onto it.

That same year, in December, another ship, the *Britomart*, bound for Hobart also shipwrecks.

She draws a ship on the wall and scrawls the words 'Britomart' onto it. She scrawls wild waves onto the wall around the ships.

That ocean sure is wild!

Mother Earth trying to tell you fullas something!

A whole year passes and the Scottish settler, so called discoverer of Gippsland, Angus McMillan ...

She sticks up a picture of Angus McMillan.

... and a couple of his stockmen are out surveying country.
Here.

She draws a Koori flag onto the wall to mark the spot.

Brataualung Country.

Just off Port Albert. Right around the corner from this motel.

That's where Aunty Ginny told me my great-great-great-grandmother Louisa got picked up and taken in by a Doctor Arbuckle after she was raped by some whitefellas. But that's another story.

McMillan spots a blackfellas camp of about twenty-five Gunaikurnai mob who quickly move off.

He reckons that as the mob are moving off, one of the women keeps looking back at him as if she's being forced away.

JACINTA *picks up a pillow from the bed and rocks it as if it's a baby ...*

McMillan also finds a kangaroo-skin bag with the dead body of a baby in it. About two years old.

He gets Doctor Arbuckle (that fulla who took in our granny Louisa) to examine the baby and he concludes—that because the flesh of the little body was discoloured; that it *probably* belonged to a white woman.

But Aunty told me that Gunaikurnai would carry our dead babies with us for weeks and months.

JACINTA *gently places the pillow back on the bed.*

Poor little fulla …

The picture of McMillan glows brighter and brighter.

So McMillan goes on his merry way, but can't stop thinking about that one woman in a possum-skin cloak that looked back at him, and that little baby in the kangaroo-skin bag.

Reckons we killed the shipwrecked survivors

Reckons we took this one white woman with us

Reckons this little dead baby is hers

Reckons our men raped her

Reckons

Reckons

Reckons …

Lights snap out on McMillan's picture in the motel room.

Cross to cop shop.

SERGEANT: Did she seem depressed or agitated to you? Anything unusual?

ROCHELLE: No. No more agitated than usual.

SERGEANT *writes in his notes*

SERGEANT: 'Signs of agitation … '

ROCHELLE: My Jacinta has gone missing! Can we get a car out to look for her now?

SERGEANT: We have to put in the paperwork.

ROCHELLE: That will take too long!

SERGEANT: Why did it take you so long to report her missing?

Beat.

ROCHELLE: Why do you reckon?

SCENE 6—MOTEL ROOM—I SAW HER

Back at the motel room. Post-it notes and highlighter markings litter the walls.

JACINTA *pins up a newspaper article.*

JACINTA: A story is sent into the papers in Melbourne about a 'kidnapped and raped white woman held captive by the Blacks' and the colonial imaginations run wild.

A gust of air rustles the Post-it notes. The walls have an opacity revealing space. A colonial GHOST appears.

GHOST: 'The idea that a female of European birth is detained in durance vile by these *ruthless savages* is horrifying in the extreme … '

JACINTA *puts her hands on the wall as if to feel a heartbeat. The GHOST disappears.*

JACINTA: On Gunaikurnai ancestral lands, shit is going down. Whitefellas are squatting everywhere, land is being cleared at an alarming rate.

She writes the name 'R. Macalister' on the wall.

A squatter by the name of Ronald Macalister has a few too many rums one night and shoots a bunch of blackfellas. Dead. More mob come back and spear and kill Macalister in retaliation. Payback.

Next day a group of squatters go out and kill one hundred and fifty Gunaikurnai in cold blood. Massacre.

She draws a squiggly line on the wall.

Right here. At Warrigal Creek.

She writes the numbers '150'.

One hundred and fifty.

She draws a skull and crossbones on the wall. The walls of the room fade again and a little boy, WILLAMBULUNG, *appears. He is shy and looks to the ground.*

They take a little Gunaikurnai orphan boy all the way to Melbourne. No mum, no dad, no brothers, no cousins, no-one. They stole him.

The squatters called the little boy 'Lively', but his tribal name is 'Willambulung' and he's got a story about this white woman.

WILLAMBULUNG *points and looks in all directions as he speaks.*

WILLAMBULUNG: I saw her washing her feet down by the river.
> I saw her with a little baby boy on her lap.
> I saw her walking along the beach.
> In a cave.
> Down the lake.
> Paddling a canoe.
> Duck diving for mussels.
> I saw her.
> I saw her.
> I saw her!

JACINTA: Poor fulla. He sure has a 'lively' imagination.
> He'd say anything for a feed.
> And to live.

There's a knock on the hotel room door and the little boy vanishes.

HOTEL MANAGER: Breakfast!

JACINTA: Shit! Is it morning already?

HOTEL MANAGER: Ms Pepper?

> *The* MANAGER *opens the door and it snags on the chain.*

> *The breakfast chute opens and the tray of food and a newspaper is delivered into the room.*

JACINTA: Mm-mm, cold toast for breakfast and the *Herald Scum*, compliments of the house.

SCENE 7—MORE SUPERVISION

SUPERVISOR'*s office.* JACINTA *enters.*

SUPERVISOR: I read your last draft.
JACINTA: And?
SUPERVISOR: What's this section here? The blacked-out bits?
JACINTA: I haven't decided whether that goes in yet.
SUPERVISOR: Why not?
JACINTA: It's secret business.
SUPERVISOR: What?
JACINTA: I've gotta talk to my Elders.
SUPERVISOR: Well, does it answer your academic question?
JACINTA: Of course it does.
SUPERVISOR: Then put it in.
JACINTA: I'm not sure yet. I don't want any more people going down to this cave. I think this should be for Gunaikurnai women's eyes only.
SUPERVISOR: Stop being so secretive. That won't help your publishing prospects.
     You have to have evidence to support your arguments. Why didn't you cite Spencer like I told you?
JACINTA: What if the archives lie? Rosaldo says 'will to truth suppresses the equally present will to power.'
SUPERVISOR: All history has happened, otherwise it wouldn't be history—it'd be a fiction. And besides, Rosaldo is an anthropologist. We are engaged in the writing of history here.
JACINTA: He's saying that the powerful can control the narrative.
SUPERVISOR: Rosaldo doesn't know whether he's an ethnographer or a poet.
JACINTA: So you've read him then?

SUPERVISOR: A little. Look, it's okay to critique and examine the archives. They're full of valuable stuff to use.

JACINTA: How valuable can they be when my people's voices are absent and the language is offensive and racist.

SUPERVISOR: The archives are an historian's primary source. They are of a time.

JACINTA: They're full of inequities. I've been looking at 'citational bias'.

SUPERVISOR: Citational justice is a fad.

JACINTA: Says who? I'm going to write my thesis without referring to any of the archives.

SUPERVISOR: What will you use then?

JACINTA: I'm going to cite Bung Yarnda.

SUPERVISOR: Who?

JACINTA: Our lake … Near my grandmother's tree.

SUPERVISOR: You can't cite an object.

JACINTA: These are not objects to us.

SUPERVISOR: A lake and a tree?

JACINTA: That lake and our birthing trees are like family.

SUPERVISOR: That's not academic. These are not literary sources.

JACINTA: They're living, breathing things that speak to us. Why can't I cite them?

SUPERVISOR: Don't be ridiculous!

JACINTA: The Maori of Aoetearoa have had their Whanganui River recognised as a legal person. 'Te Awa Tupua': The River Claims Settlement Act.

SUPERVISOR: A river is a river. Not a person.

JACINTA: But it is to us.

SUPERVISOR: Have you considered writing a novel or going for a journalism cadetship?

JACINTA: What?

SUPERVISOR: It'd make good use of the material you've gathered thus far.

JACINTA: The material? This is deeply considered research.
      I want to be an historian.

SUPERVISOR: Why?

JACINTA: Because 'White Australia Has a Black History'.

SUPERVISOR: Your thesis has to be more than a T-shirt slogan Jacinta.

JACINTA: Doctor Romaine Moreton says:

'The struggle for Indigenous writers is that not only must we write in order to move towards that space beyond western language, but that it is necessary to enter into a 'war of fictions' so that we may be free of it.'

SUPERVISOR: You have two days to submit your proposal before you launch into World War Three. This is a university, not a battleground.

JACINTA: Is it?

Beat.

SUPERVISOR: You've got two days.

The figure of the WHITE WOMAN *in possum-skin cloak walks by.* JACINTA *follows her.*

SCENE 8—MOTEL ROOM—HISTORY REPEATING

JACINTA *paces in a rage. A distant figure of the* WHITE WOMAN *in possum-skin cloak appears through the walls.*

JACINTA: Nobody hears or sees the White Woman for three whole years and the wild frontier continues to rage. Gunaikurnai are killing the sheep and the squatters are killing the Gunaikurnai.

Two TROOPERS *appear in silhouette and stalk the* WHITE WOMAN.

They use blackfella troopers from the next-door mob to try and control us.

Jacky Jackies
Doing the white man's work
Puffed up
Riding horses
Getting a feed
Reckons they saw that white woman
Reckons she wore a possum-skin cloak
Reckons she ran
Reckons she dropped her cloak
In the swamp
Reckons

Reckons
Reckons
'No boss, we saw her
That yellow woman
We saw her'
Sniff that cloak
With their Jacky Jacky noses
'Yes boss, smell like a white woman wore this cloak.'
'Good boy
Good boy'

The figure of the WHITE WOMAN *in possum-skin cloak and the two* TROOPERS *disappear.*

How do we know they weren't just wanting revenge on us Gunaikurnai in retaliation for past wars? Why are these Native Police trooping around on Gunaikurnai land anyway!? Who is this 'yellow woman'? And if she wanted to be rescued why did she run away?

She sticks up an archival picture of a Gunaikurnai warrior on the wall and writes the words 'Bungelene/Bunjil-ene' in firm bold texta.

The whitefellas have heard about a big man called Bungelene (*'boon-jool-eenee'*). They call him 'a chief'. But Aunty Ginny told me that any man with a 'bunjil' (*'boon-jool'*) before his name is a lore man.

She underlines the word bunjil three or four times.

A clever man. A medicine man. Bungelene is six foot tall with a big grey beard and they reckon he's got that White Woman for one of his wives.

JACINTA *gets a reward notice and sticks it up on the wall. Wind rustles the Post-it notes and* DE VILLIERS' *ghost appears.* TROOPERS *nail handkerchiefs onto trees. We hear the intermittent staccato of hammers on nails.*

Governor LaTrobe posts a one-thousand-pound reward and another search party from Melbourne is formed; this one led by Christian de Villiers,

She puts up a picture of Christian de Villiers.

James Warman, four other white fullas and ten blackfullas from the next-door mob.

They nail handkerchiefs onto the trees and place them on the leaves and branches of low-lying bushes.

On each handkerchief is a neatly printed message in English on one side and Gaelic on the other:

DE VILLIERS *appears.*

DE VILLIERS: 'WHITE WOMAN! There are fourteen armed men, partly White and partly Black, in search of you. Be cautious; and rush to them when you see them near you. Be particularly on the lookout every dawn of morning, for it is then that the party are in hopes of rescuing you. The white settlement is towards the setting sun.'

She draws the route of two boats on the lake and an 'X' where they land.

JACINTA: The expedition party take two whale boats up the lakes and land on the edge of Lake Victoria at a place called Golgatha where they see the abandoned fires of the Gunaikurnai. There are bones and dead people everywhere.

WILLAMBULANG *and* DANCER *appear, defending country.*

These Melbourne toffs have arrived smack bang in the middle of a war zone …

DE VILLIERS: ' … truly a fine race of athletic savages … (but) the settlers think no more of shooting them than they do of eating their dinners … From all I can see and hear … the Worrigals' extermination will at no very distant day be accomplished, as all intercourse with them is with powder and ball.'

DE VILLIERS *brings his gun up and points it at* WILLAMBULUNG.

JACINTA: No!

There's a knock on the breakfast hatch and it opens, letting in the piercing white light of the day. DE VILLIERS *and* WILLAMBULUNG *disappear. A breakfast tray and newspaper is pushed in and the hatch closes abruptly.*

Shit. I need some sleep.

SCENE 9—MORE COP SHOP

Back at the police station. AUNTY ROCHELLE *sits waiting.* JACINTA'*s image in the hotel room overlaps and gently fades.* SERGEANT *enters with paperwork.*

SERGEANT: I've run a check on your niece to see if anything comes up.

ROCHELLE: What in the hell do you think is gonna come up?

SERGEANT: It's standard procedure.

ROCHELLE: I've put notices up at the health and legal service. Rung all her friends. The university. No-one's seen her. What have you been doing?

SERGEANT: We're doing the best we can.

ROCHELLE: I'm going crazy while you're here pushing paper around!

SERGEANT: I can refer you to a counselling service.

ROCHELLE: Like the service you provided for my sister?

> *Beat.*

SERGEANT: We're not here to talk about Leanne.

ROCHELLE: You're on a first-name basis now?

SERGEANT: No.

ROCHELLE: I'm surprised you remember her name.

SERGEANT: I went to school with your sister …

ROCHELLE: Ah, that's right.

> *Beat.*

SERGEANT: Look, Rochelle I'm / sorry—

ROCHELLE: I just want you to put out a missing persons report.

> *Silence.*

> SERGEANT *types.*

SERGEANT: How's Kyle going?

> *Beat.*

I saw him down the street with some boys the other day having a bit of a lark.

ROCHELLE: Oh yeah. And? Is having a 'lark' a crime?

SERGEANT: There's a few boys been getting into a bit of trouble lately and wherever they go, there's been a bit of stealing.

ROCHELLE: Yeah, he told me you stopped and checked his school bag.

SERGEANT: Got a bit of a mouth on him, your son.

ROCHELLE: Maybe you should keep your eyes off our Black kids and go check out those McKenzie boys.

SERGEANT: Right.

Beat.

And how's his dad going?

ROCHELLE: Why do you want to know?

SERGEANT: Heard he's back in jail.

Silence.

SERGEANT *types.*

ROCHELLE: Your daughter was in the same year as Jacinta?

SERGEANT: That's right.

Silence.

SERGEANT *types.*

ROCHELLE: Heard she got married.

SERGEANT: That's right.

ROCHELLE: Musta been nice walking your daughter down the aisle?

SERGEANT: Yes, it was.

ROCHELLE: Seeing your son graduate.

SERGEANT: Yeah.

ROCHELLE: You must be real proud.

SERGEANT: I am.

ROCHELLE: He in the policing business too?

SERGEANT: He is, as a matter of fact. Same academy as me.

Silence.

ROCHELLE: And you got a promotion.

Beat.

SERGEANT: Yes, I did.

ROCHELLE: Senior sergeant.

SERGEANT: That's correct.

ROCHELLE: Even after you went on all that post-traumatic stress leave.

SERGEANT: That's enough!

ROCHELLE: Another stripe on your arm and a feather in your cap.

SERGEANT: We did a thorough internal investigation and we've acted on the recommendations.

ROCHELLE: I reckon my sister would've liked to see her daughter graduate.

SERGEANT: I said that's enough!

> ROCHELLE *stands to leave.*

I'm just waiting for the results of the check on your niece and then we can post the missing persons report. It's …

ROCHELLE: … standard procedure. I know …

> *The* SERGEANT *points to the chair.* ROCHELLE *reluctantly takes a seat.*

SCENE 10—REMEMBERING

JACINTA *sits on the end of her bed. A beam of sunlight streaks into the motel room. A magpie warbles.*

JACINTA: You were in the kitchen.

> Boiled the kettle
> Put the bread and vegemite
> On the bench
> Said

> 'Sorry, there's not much for lunch today.
> Pay day next week.
> Just gotta get through the weekend.'

> And you wrapped your
> Blue dressing gown around you
> Got up and leaned against
> The kitchen sink.

> I didn't clock it then

> You were looking at the sun
> Coming through the window
> You were bathed in this beautiful golden light

Beams of light
Hitting the sink and up onto your face

And this magpie
Landed on the fence
He was serenading you.

And you said,

'See Old Man Magpie.
He looking for a feed.
We got nothing!
You beautiful boy.'

You laughed
With all that sun on your face

Then I walked out the door
And you shouted
'You be good now!
Don't do anything I wouldn't do.'
I held up my hand.
Didn't look back.
That magpie warbled.
A warning.
He knew.
They were coming for ya.

SCENE 11—COP SHOP AGAIN

The cop shop. ROCHELLE *waits. Foot tapping.* SERGEANT *finally enters. He passes a photograph to* ROCHELLE.

SERGEANT: Can you verify if this is Jacinta in this photo?
ROCHELLE: What is this?
SERGEANT: It's from a speed camera.
ROCHELLE: I can see that.
SERGEANT: Is this her car?
ROCHELLE: Yes.
SERGEANT: She'll have to pay a fine.
ROCHELLE: When was this taken?
SERGEANT: About four weeks ago.

ROCHELLE: No. No. No.

SERGEANT: The car's unregistered.

ROCHELLE: What!?

SERGEANT: Are you aware she has unpaid fines?

ROCHELLE: This is a missing persons report, not a criminal check.

SERGEANT: That makes a lot of sense.

ROCHELLE: What sense?

SERGEANT: This happens all the time.

ROCHELLE: I know exactly where this is going.

SERGEANT: Young women do something wrong and then they go …

ROCHELLE: Go on, say it.

SERGEANT: I'm just saying, this is a pattern. We see this all the time …

ROCHELLE: Go on, say it.

SERGEANT: Say what?

RROCHELLE: ' … And then they go … ' Walkabout?

SERGEANT: Away! They go away!

ROCHELLE: Get your grubby eyes off my niece!

SERGEANT: Well then, she should've paid her car fine.

ROCHELLE *pushes the* SERGEANT *and gets in his face.*

ROCHELLE: Don't you dare!

SERGEANT: Calm down.

ROCHELLE: You don't get to do this again.

SERGEANT: Everyone has to abide by the law.

ROCHELLE: You've got nothing better to do than chase women around for car fines?

SERGEANT: Take a seat.

ROCHELLE: What a big man you are.

SERGEANT: Do you want me to file this missing persons report or not?

ROCHELLE: So you can throw my niece in the lock up because of a car fine? That's a death sentence.

SERGEANT: I'm just doing my job.

ROCHELLE: Do you hose out the police cells at night? Is that your job too?

SERGEANT: Rochelle, I can see you're upset.

ROCHELLE: Don't use your calming technique bullshit on me.

SERGEANT: Now, come on …

ROCHELLE: Did you use that technique on my sister too?

SERGEANT: Your sister was no saint, Rochelle.

ROCHELLE: You hounded her!

SERGEANT: Your sister was a drunk.

> ROCHELLE *grabs him by the collar.*

ROCHELLE: My sister got thrown in the cell for being poor and Black. She never hurt a soul.

SERGEANT: Let go of me, Rochelle.

ROCHELLE: Just another drunk. Another Black. Another troublemaker. Another 'boong'.

SERGEANT: Do you want me to file this missing persons report or …

ROCHELLE: Or what?

> ROCHELLE *lets him go and goes to slap him across the face. She doesn't make contact, but he flinches just the same.*
>
> *They face off.*

I'll find her myself.

> ROCHELLE *exits.*

SCENE 12—PROCRASTINATION BLUES

JACINTA*'s room in the deep dark middle of the night.* JACINTA *is resolutely awake.*

She handballs her stress ball against the wall, looking for answers.

Blackout.

JACINTA *stares at the telly blankly, changing the channels.*

Blackout.

She squeezes the stress ball vociferously and stares at the wall still looking for answers.

Blackout.

The laptop is the only light in the room. JACINTA *paces, sits at her laptop, paces again, sits.*

Blackout.

JACINTA *grabs her thesis and throws it against the wall. Papers scatter everywhere.*

She sits and puts her head in her hands. DANCER *appears and picks up the pieces of paper. One by one.*

SCENE 13—EMPTY CARAVAN

AUNTY ROCHELLE *sits alone in the caravan, staring into space. She dials Jacinta's phone number and we hear the answerphone message.* KYLE *enters.*

JACINTA: [*voiceover*]
    Look up my people
    The Dawn is breaking
    The world is waking
    To a new bright day

    When none defame us
    No restriction tame us
    Nor colour shame us
    Nor sneer dismay

    Now brood no more
    On the years behind you
    The hope assigned you
    Shall the past replace

    When a juster justice
    Grown wise and stronger
    Points the bone no longer
    At a darker race ...

Get my message?
    You know what to do...
    The phone beeps to receive a message and ROCHELLE *hangs up.*

ROCHELLE: It's an Oodgeroo Noonuccal poem. She had it stuck above
    her bedhead when she was a teenager.
KYLE: She still not picking up?
    You should go back to bed.

ROCHELLE: I'll be right.

> KYLE *sits with his mum.*

KYLE: Do you reckon she'll come back?

ROCHELLE: Yeah. She'll come back.

> *Pause.*

KYLE: Why is she doing all this study? It looks like hell.

ROCHELLE: She's trying to make sense of the world, son.

KYLE: Yeah, but it looks like torture.

> *Beat.*

Remember that set of encyclopedias you got her one Christmas?

ROCHELLE: [*chuckling*] Yeah.

KYLE: Those little sparkly purple ones.

ROCHELLE: Cost me a fortune. Got my money's worth though. She read those books from A to Z and then started from A again …

KYLE: Even took them with her when we went camping that time.

ROCHELLE: Yep. She brought K, L, M and N with her!

KYLE: Sat under that big gumtree with her nose in those books and couldn't get a peep out of her. Wouldn't go swimming or fishing or nothing.

ROCHELLE: She was a bookworm, alright.

KYLE: Why is she doing this?

ROCHELLE: She wants to make things better.

KYLE: In this shithole town?

> *Pause.*

Sometimes you can know too much, ay?

ROCHELLE: Yeah. Maybe you're right.

> *Beat.*

KYLE: I'm sorry I got her in trouble for not picking me up.

ROCHELLE: It's not your fault.

KYLE: Yeah, but what if she doesn't come back?

ROCHELLE: She'll come back.

KYLE: I reckon I need to know more.

ROCHELLE: I reckon I need to know more too.

KYLE: I reckon this whole country needs to know more.

ROCHELLE: I reckon too.

Pause.

KYLE: You don't think she …

ROCHELLE: She'll come back. I know she will.

SCENE 14—MOTEL DREAMING

JACINTA *is finally asleep … sort of … She tosses and turns. The* WHITE WOMAN *in possum-skin cloak enters and sits on the end of* JACINTA's *bed.* JACINTA *wakes.*

JACINTA: Maybe you never wanted to be found?

> Your feet on our ground
> Our scars on your chest
> Your hair woven
> Into string nets and baskets
> Your children fat-bellied
>
> A cave and a possum-skin cloak
> Your new home.
>
> Maybe you preferred
> The 'wildness' of the Blacks?
>
> Are you a figment?
> A whiff of mist?
> A puff of white magic?
>
> Someone to rescue?
> A damsel in distress?

The WHITE WOMAN *is walking, fading away.*

Who are you?

> Did you like us?
>
> Did you love us?
>
> Who are you?
>
> Are you even there?

She follows the WHITE WOMAN.

SCENE 15—THE STORM

WILLAMBULUNG *appears in the room. A storm is brewing.*

WILLAMBULUNG: Hey, djidyarn (*sister*).

> *He hands* JACINTA *the pages of her thesis as he speaks.* JACINTA *sits up.*

JACINTA: Who? …

WILLAMBULUNG: Djidyarn!

JACINTA: What? …

WILLAMBULUNG: It's Willambulung.

> Those whitefellas
> Been looking for that old man
> Bungelene (*boon-jool-eenee*)
> Clever man
>
> I take them to him

> *The* DANCER *enters as* BUNGELENE. *Shapeshifting and channelling his spirit now.*

He's our lore man
> Bungelene speaks to them whitefellas.
> Big talk
>
> Reckons he took that White Woman
> Reckons he's got her hidden
> Reckons she's got his baby
>
> Reckons
> Reckons
> Reckons
>
> They march us up and down
> Hills mountains rivers lakes
> Looking for this one White Woman
>
> And us blackfellas
> we just keep telling them
>
> Yes boss, that white woman, she's over there.

She's at the women's camp.

Down the river

With my brother, down on the island.

Up in a cave

Whatever they want to hear.
Get them the hell off our land.

They drag us down to the island.
Nothing.
No White Woman.

Those white fullas
Getting real prickly now.

They say,

DE VILLIERS *appears.*

DE VILLIERS: 'You bring this woman now!
You bring her or we'll come back
with more men and more guns.'

WILLAMBULUNG: Old man Bungelene
Getting real wild.
He wants to flog them fellas
but I say,

No Uncle. Be careful. Them fellas are bad.

More whitefellas come
with more men and more guns

Take Bungelene
to that government fella
Make him sign this paper.
Here. This one here.

WILLAMBULUNG *hands* JACINTA *the agreement.*

DE VILLIERS *and* BUNGELENE *appear.*

DE VILLIERS: 'I, Bungelene, promise to deliver to Charles J. Tyers the
white female residing with the Gipps Land Blacks …

I also agree to leave my two wives and two children with the
said Charles J. Tyers as hostages for the fulfillment of my promise.'

JACINTA: No!!!

WILLAMBULUNG: Put that old man's finger in the ink
Make him sign like this

> WILLAMBULUNG *marks an 'x' in the air.* DE VILLIERS *puts* BUNGELENE's *finger in an ink pot.*

JACINTA: No! These are not his words. He doesn't know what you're saying!

> JACINTA *grabs* BUNGELENE's *agreement, screws up the piece of paper and throws it in the bin. Tries to stop* BUNGELENE *from signing the agreement.*

No. Stop. Stop!
Because we all know
Where this is going
Don't we?

> DE VILLIERS *chains up* BUNGELENE.

WILLAMBULUNG: Take him to the police yard.
His two wives too.

JACINTA: No.

WILLAMBULUNG: Chain him to that tree.

Longest time.

Too long.

For eighteen months.

They tortured him.

We heard the women wail.

JACINTA: No, no, no.

WILLAMBULUNG: Bungelene …
Our Clever Man.

JACINTA: No!

> *Lights fade out on* BUNGELENE.

> *Pause.*

WILLAMBULUNG: Poor fulla.

> *Beat.*

JACINTA: Our first Black Death in custody.

Ground Zero.

A strong wind whips up, billowing the curtains and blowing JACINTA*'s thesis around the room. Majestic and eerie.*

Flashes of ghosts appear ...

DE VILLIERS *with his gun pointed. Blackout.*

The WHITE WOMAN *walking through the forest. Blackout.*

The Black TROOPERS *nailing handkerchiefs onto the branches. Blackout.*

WILLAMBULUNG *calling 'Hey djidyarn.' Blackout.*

A breakfast tray shoved through the hatch. Blackout.

The WHITE WOMAN *revealed as* JACINTA*'s mother. Blackout.*

The DANCER, *dressed in full regalia and painted to the max like a proper Gunaikurnai warrior. Blackout.*

Another breakfast tray shoved in, then another and another and another. Blackout.

The SERGEANT *mopping up a cell with blue gloves on. Blackout.*

Frenzied now, JACINTA *tears the papers off the wall.*

No!

I'm not writing history anymore
You use your words against us
No!

I'm writing the truth.

She rips up the archive books and newspapers and throws them into the bin.

No more lies!

I'm not following this paper trail anymore.

It's killing us!

No!

She throws the candle into the bin and the papers catch fire.

She tips the entire contents of the archive box into the bin and the flames grow higher.

Papers fly around the room like a flock of corellas.

The DANCER *is singing up magic now and the country replies.*

SCENE 16—READING THE COUNTRY

The walls of the motel room disappear. WILLAMBULUNG *beckons.*
JACINTA *is drawn deep inside a Gunaikurnai forest.*

WILLAMBULUNG: Didjiyarn, here! Come on!
JACINTA: My foot falls
    Where theirs have been

    Through the ferns
    Under giant trees
    Vibrant silver
    They stand guard

    The earth is soft and spongy
    She holds me now
    One foot in front of the other

    And I follow
    I am warm

    And my guide leads me
WILLAMBULUNG: Come on. Come on, didjiyarn
JACINTA: Familiar country
    DNA memories
    Ingrained
WILLAMBULUNG: Come on now …
JACINTA: We walk.
    Rest at the crystal clear creek
    She sustains us.

    Lower my face, my lips
    Kiss the water.
    I drink.

    Willambulung feeds me
    Kangaroo and some stolen sheep
    Cheeky bugger
WILLAMBULUNG: He good one that Baaaaaah Baaaaaah

JACINTA: We laugh and chew
Laugh and chew

Willambulung, he says,
WILLAMBULUNG: What you doin here?
JACINTA: I tell him.
This is my Mother's country.
My yackan.

This isn't written in the books

I'm reading the country now

Willambulung is getting faster.

Faster, faster

A shotgun blasts

Stops us in our tracks.
WILLAMBULUNG: Whetpella!
JACINTA: They've seen our smoke.
Followed our tracks

He takes me by the arm
Picks up his pace

Through the swamp
Where they found her cloak

Around the shores of the lake
See the whitefellas' boats parked there

We count their footprints
Ten.

Ten men on our tail.
They looking for that white woman too.

Hear the guns
WILLAMBULUNG: 'Boo! Boo!'
JACINTA: Faster. Faster now.
We hear the sea

Climb the giant dunes
Waves roar
Louder.
Louder now.

Sea mist hits our faces
Powerful
And frightening

WILLAMBULUNG: Nark-abun-dhu.

JACINTA: We're at the back of the world

WILLAMBULUNG *points.*

WILLAMBULUNG: Mandha Taba taba maian. (*There white woman/wife.*)

JACINTA: There, that's where we saw her.

WILLAMBULUNG *starts to sing and dance, slow and hard. The* DANCER *accompanies him.*

Willambulung starts singing
His voice comes up from the core of the earth
Soft and low and powerful

WILLAMBULUNG: Gillwurt! …

JACINTA: … he says,

WILLAMBULUNG: Gillwurt!

JACINTA: And we get down on our knees
And dig

That sand
She's cold on my knees

WILLAMBULUNG: Gillwurt!

JACINTA: And we dig.

Willambulang sings louder now
Drowns out the drone of the sea

He sees the whitefellas coming
Doesn't care

WILLAMBULUNG: Gillwurt!

JACINTA: Our hands hit something solid

We squat and wait for the earth
To give birth

Pushes me out of the way

He pulls up that white woman!

WILLAMBULUNG: Lohan Tuka

JACINTA: Takes her now
　　　From that secret sacred
　　　Place

　　　Holds her gently.
　　　Wipes the sand from her
　　　Hair.
　　　Her face.
　　　Her eyes.

　　　Pause.

WILLAMBULUNG: This woman.
　　　She magic.

　　　She come onto the beach
　　　She lay here for a real long time
　　　And we try to work out her story
　　　We been singing to her
　　　But she say nothing
　　　She got no song.

　　　She come to us.
　　　We don't know why

　　　But we take good care of her.

JACINTA: White Woman stands tall
　　　Shows us her fishy tail
　　　Her hard wooden breasts
　　　The trident in her hand

　　　The figurehead of the HMS *Britannia*

　　　A wooden carving.

　　　To us, she was sacred.

　　　When they asked us, if we had the White Woman
　　　Yes, we did.

　　　This is your 'White Woman of Gippsland'
　　　Here she is …
　　　Maybe.

SCENE 17—BEACH CELL

BLACKFELLAS 1, 2 *and* 3 *stand on a wild and rugged beach. The* SERGEANT *stands to one side. He is not of their world.*

BLACKFELLA 1: A grey blanket
BLACKFELLA 2: A mound
BLACKFELLA 3: Not moving
BLACKFELLA 1: A pile of flesh
    And bones
BLACKFELLA 2: Held together with love and loss
SERGEANT: When I went in there
    I could see something wasn't right.
BLACKFELLA 1: She went in for parking fines.
SERGEANT: Something isn't right
BLACKFELLA 2: On the windscreen
SERGEANT: Her face has gone grey.
BLACKFELLA 3: Flapping in the breeze
SERGEANT: I call out to her.
    Leanne?
BLACKFELLA 2: Her hand reaching out
    for a puffer
BLACKFELLA 3: That never came
BLACKFELLA 1: She called out to you.
    'I have asthma.
    I can't breathe.
    I need my puffer.'
SERGEANT: Leanne?
BLACKFELLA 2: Lips blue
BLACKFELLA 3: Eyes wide
    In fright
BLACKFELLA 1: Nobody came.
SERGEANT: Leanne. Leanne!
BLACKFELLA 1: Until it was too late.
BLACKFELLA 2: Can't breathe, can't talk
SERGEANT: Put on the blue gloves.
    Step in a few steps closer.

BLACKFELLA 1: She gets up
BLACKFELLA 3: Falls
BLACKFELLA 1: Gets up again …
BLACKFELLA 2: Can't breathe, can't talk
SERGEANT: She's fallen
BLACKFELLA 1: Legs give way
BLACKFELLA 2: Not enough air
BLACKFELLA 3: Can't keep upright
SERGEANT: Bloody drunken Abo …
BLACKFELLA 3: Back to bed, back to bed
BLACKFELLA 1: Under the blanket
BLACKFELLA 3: She's cold.
SERGEANT: When did we check her last?
    Check the logbook.
BLACKFELLA 1: So cold.
BLACKFELLA 2: Stinging scratchy itchy
BLACKFELLA 1: She pulls at her T-shirt
SERGEANT: Press on her arm
    With my latex-covered fingers
    There's drool on her chin.
BLACKFELLA 3: Mouth agape
BLACKFELLA 1: Willing her lungs to fill
SERGEANT: Fuck! Wake up! Wake up!
BLACKFELLA 1: Lungs on fire
BLACKFELLA 3: Neck outstretched
BLACKFELLA 2: Gasping for air
BLACKFELLA 1: She wants air!
SERGEANT: Nothing
BLACKFELLA 1: Breath gets shorter
    Faster
    In, out. In …
BLACKFELLA 2: Won't go out
SERGEANT: Roll her on her side!
BLACKFELLA 1: Breath won't go out.
SERGEANT: I can't remember whether we logged on our last check.
BLACKFELLA 2: Breath gets shorter
    Faster
    In out in …

BLACKFELLA 3: Won't go out
BLACKFELLA 2: Shoulders rise and fall
BLACKFELLA 1: Rise and fall
SERGEANT: Fuck! Call an ambulance.
BLACKFELLA 1: Tired, tired now.

BLACKFELLA 3: So so tired

BLACKFELLA 1: Disoriented dizzy

BLACKFELLA 3: Heavy chest
SERGEANT: No need for flashing lights.

BLACKFELLA 2: A bloody stone.
SERGEANT: This isn't an emergency

BLACKFELLA 1: No words now
SERGEANT: This is a morgue job.

BLACKFELLA 2: Eyes closed
BLACKFELLA 3: Heavy so heavy

BLACKFELLA 1: Mum?
SERGEANT: Fuck!

BLACKFELLA 3: Nothing
BLACKFELLA 1: Mum!
SERGEANT: All hands on deck
        For the clean-up.
        We're not going to get home before dawn.

ALL: Gone.

BLACKFELLA 1: She's gone.

The wind and sea rages. The sky turns Blak with rage.
AUNTY ROCHELLE *and* KYLE *hug* JACINTA. *Tight and long.*
A homecoming.
The DANCER *performs a smoking ceremony.*
It is a cleansing. A healing.

EPILOGUE: THE DEADLY FUTURE

JACINTA *is smartly dressed and stands at a lectern.*

'12th INTERNATIONAL SYMPOSIUM
ON CULTURE AND HISTORY
KEYNOTE ADDRESS:
'The Black Women of Gippsland: When history lives in you.'
by Doctor Jacinta Pepper'
is projected behind her.

JACINTA: Once upon a time there was a woman.
A White Woman.
She got washed ashore
And we rescued her.
Or we trapped her.
Or we impregnated her
Or we adopted her
Or we killed her
Or we ate her
Or we loved her
Or we never saw her.

They spent all this time and money looking for a white woman
I reckon she was never there.

This paper is a contribution to the international discourse on first contact histories. It centres community based oral histories that question historical archives that are colonially biased.

As a Gunaikurnai historian how am I expected to reference an archive that is racist and dehumanising?

Writing in 1857, Henry Gyles Turner, (colonial banker and historian) called the so called 'White Woman of Gippsland',

' ... a poor fluttering pigeon in a nest of vultures ... '

and my people, The Gunaikurnai,

' ... a horde of the most debased and degraded savages ... '

I went looking for this 'White Woman of Gippsland ... '

Like everybody else has been looking for her...

But who are the women who are really missing and dying?

You live on my Mother's country as if nothing happened. You are willfully blind to the truth and we must change the dominant discourse. It is deathly.

I dedicate this paper to Bungelene [boon-jool-eenee] and his two wives, who were tied to a tree for eighteen months at the Narre Warren police yard in 1846 as hostages for a white woman who never was.

One of his wives was named was Parley. The other was un-named. She died in police custody too. The colonists didn't bother to record her name.

Why?

Because she was a Black Woman.

If you are a Blackfella in this country you are twelve times more likely to be imprisoned, and if you are a Black woman, you are twenty times more likely....

There have been five hundred and eighty-eight[*] Black Deaths in Custody since the Royal Commission into Black Deaths in 1991.

I dedicate this paper to the thousands of Black women around the world who have died and gone missing since colonisation.

I dedicate this paper to the memory of my mother Leanne Lyn Pepper who died in police custody on the 13th December 2014.

She was....

The Black Woman of Gippsland

JACINTA *returns to the Gunaikurnai rainforest.*

Gunaikurnai country has the last word.
Lights fade to black.

THE END

---

*Tragically … it will be necessary to update this number at time of production.

NEXT STAGE

Commissioned and developed through Melbourne Theatre Company's NEXT STAGE Writers' Program with the support of our Current and Inaugural Playwrights Giving Circles.

NEXT STAGE positions new Australian works as contenders on the national stage, through strategic investment in stories that reflect our community, are relevant to our times, challenge the boundaries of theatre making and fuel the cultural conversation.

Thank you for sharing our passion and commitment to Australian stories and Australian writers.

PLAYWRIGHTS GIVING CIRCLE

Thank you to Melbourne Theatre Company's Playwrights Giving Circle – its donors, foundations and organisations – for sharing our passion and commitment to Australian stories and writers.

Fitzpatrick Sykes Family Foundation, The Glenholme Foundation, Jane Hansen AO and Paul Little AO, Larry Kamener and Petra Kamener, Susanna Mason, Helen Nicolay, Pimlico Foundation, Tania Seary and Chris Lynch, Craig Semple, Dr Richard Simmie, Andrew Sisson AO and Tracey Sisson, Derek and Caroline Young

MALCOLM ROBERTSON FOUNDATION   The Vizard FOUNDATION

INAUGURAL PLAYWRIGHTS GIVING CIRCLE

Louise Myer & Martyn Myer AO, Maureen Wheeler AO & Tony Wheeler AO, Christine Brown Bequest, Allan Myers AC KC & Maria Myers AC, Tony Burgess & Janine Burgess, Dr Andrew McAliece & Dr Richard Simmie, Larry Kamener & Petra Kamener

The Ian Potter Foundation   NAOMI MILGROM FOUNDATION   THE MYER FOUNDATION   MALCOLM ROBERTSON FOUNDATION   THE UNIVERSITY OF MELBOURNE

Melbourne Theatre Company

Our Donors

We gratefully acknowledge the ongoing support of our leading Donors.

LIFETIME PATRONS

Acknowledging a lifetime of extraordinary support.

Rowland Ball OAM &
   The Late Monica Maughan
Pat Burke
Peter Clemenger AO &
   The Late Joan Clemenger AO
Greig Gailey &
   Dr Geraldine Lazarus

Allan Myers AC KC &
   Maria Myers AC
The Late Biddy Ponsford
The Late Dr Roger Riordan AM
Maureen Wheeler AO &
   Tony Wheeler AO

The Late Ursula Whiteside
Caroline Young &
   Derek Young AM

ENDOWMENT FUND DONORS

Supporting Melbourne Theatre Company's long-term sustainability and creative future.

Leading Gifts

Jane Hansen AO & Paul Little AO
The Late Max Schultz &
   The Late Jill Schultz
The University of Melbourne

$50,000+

The Late Margaret Anne Brien
Tony & Janine Burgess
John Higgins AO &
   Jodie Maunder
Martin & Loreto Hosking
The Late Valerie Gwendolyn King
The Late Biddy Ponsford
Andrew Sisson AO &
   Tracey Sisson
The Late Geoffrey Cohen AM
The John & Myriam Wylie
   Foundation

$20,000+

Robert A. Dunster
Prudence & Neil Morrison
Tania Seary & Chris Lynch

$10,000+

Helen Lynch AM & Helen Bauer
Jennifer Darbyshire &
   David Walker
Charles Gilles & Penny Allen
Ian Hicks AO
Tony & Nathalie Johnson
Jane Kunstler
Craig Semple

PLAYWRIGHTS GIVING CIRCLE

Supporting the NEXT STAGE Writers' Program, our industry-leading commissioning initiative.

Fitzpatrick Sykes Family Foundation, The Glenholme Foundation, Jane Hansen AO and Paul Little AO, Larry Kamener and Petra Kamener, Susanna Mason, Helen Nicolay, Pimlico Foundation, Tania Seary and Chris Lynch, Craig Semple, Dr Richard Simmie, Andrew Sisson AO and Tracey Sisson, Derek and Caroline Young

MALCOLM ROBERTSON FOUNDATION   The Vizard FOUNDATION

TRUSTS & FOUNDATIONS

Cybec Foundation   The Gailey Lazarus Foundation   HANSEN LITTLE FOUNDATION   The Ian Potter Foundation   ROBERT SALZER FOUNDATION

trawalla foundation   NEWSBOYS FOUNDATION   JOHN & MYRIAM Wylie   VICTORIA State Government

Annual giving

Acknowledging Donors whose recent gifts help enrich and transform lives through the magic of theatre.

Current as of April 2025.

BENEFACTORS CIRCLE

$50,000+

The Late Margaret Anne Brian
Tony & Janine Burgess
Krystyna Campbell-Pretty AM
Peter Clemenger AO
Greig Gaily &
  Dr Geraldine Lazarus
Jane Hansen AO & Paul Little AO

John Higgins AO & Jodie Maunder
Martin & Loreto Hosking
The Late Valerie Gwendolyn King
The Late Max &
  the Late Jill Schultz
Tania Seary & Chris Lynch
Fitzpatrick Sykes Family

Foundation
Maureen Wheeler AO &
  Tony Wheeler AO
The John & Myriam Wylie
  Foundation

$20,000+

Jay Bethell & Peter Smart
Linda Herd
Petra & Larry Kamener
Ian & Margaret McKellar

Prudence & Neil Morrison
Craig Semple
Andrew Sisson AO &
  Tracey Sisson

The John & Myriam Wylie
  Foundation
Anonymous (1)

$10,000+

Alan & Mary-Louise
  Archibald Foundation
APS Foundation
John & Lorraine Bates
Joanna Baevski
Jay Bethell & Peter Smart
Michael Buxton AM &
  Janet Buxton
Kathleen Canfell
Angie & Colin Carter
The Cattermole Family
Jennifer Darbyshire &
  David Walker

The Dowd Foundation
Charles Gilles & Penny Allen
Charles & Cornelia
  Goode Foundation
John & Joan Grigg OAM
Ian Hicks AO
Diane John
Tony & Nathalie Johnson
Petra & Larry Kamener
Helen Lynch AM & Helen Bauer
Susanna Mason
MRB Foundation
Helen Nicolay

Pimlico Foundation
Catherine Quealy
Janet Reid OAM & Allan Reid
Lisa Ring
Anne & Mark Robertson OAM
Dr Richard Simmie
Rob Stewart & Lisa Dowd
Tintagel Bay P/L
Ralph Ward-Ambler AM &
  Barbara Ward-Ambler
Matt Williams – Artem Group
Anonymous (2)

$5,000+

Bagôt Gjergja Foundation
James Best & Doris Young
Paul & Wendy Bonnici & Family
Bowness Family Foundation
Dr Douglas Brown &
  Treena Brown
Dr Andrew Buchanan &
  Peter Darcy
Ian & Jillian Buchanan
Bill Burdett AM & Sandra Burdett
Pat Burke & Jan Nolan
Diana Burleigh
Alison & John Cameron
Ann Cutts
Prof Glyn Davis AC &
  Prof Margaret Gardner AC
Marian Evans

Melody & Jonathan Feder
Christine Gilbertson
Roger & Jan Goldsmith
Lesley Griffin
David & Lily Harris
Jane Hemstritch AO
Tony Hillery &
  Warwick Eddington
Bruce & Mary Humphries
Sam & Jacky Hupert
Dr Sonay Hussein, in memory
  of Prof David Penington AC
Karen Inge & Dr George Janko
Amy & Paul Jasper
Daryl Kendrick &
  Leong Lai Peng (Betty)
Josephine & Graham Kraehe AO

Jane Kunstler
Martin & Melissa McIntosh
Kim & Peter Monk
George & Rosa Morstyn
The Myer Foundation
Tom & Ruth O'Dea
Leigh O'Neill
Roger & Ruth Parker
Dr Kia Pajouhesh
  (Smile Solutions)
Renzella Family
Lynne Sherwood
Geoffrey Smith & Gary Singer
Trawalla Foundation Trust
Janet Whiting AM & Phil Lukies
Rebecca Wilkinson
Anonymous (4)

ADVOCATES CIRCLE

$2,500+

Ros Boyce
Paul & Robyn Brasher
Nigel & Sheena Broughton
Nan Brown
Lynne & Rob Burgess
Geoff Cosgriff
Susanne Dahn
Ann Darby
Megan Davis & Antony Isaacson
Kaye and John de Wijn
Rodney Dux
Anna & John Field
Nigel & Cathy Garrard
Diana & Murray Gerstman

Heather & Bob Glindemann OAM
Henry Gold
Jane Grover
Halina Lewenberg Charitable
    Foundation
Peter & Halina Jacobsen
Professor Duncan Maskell &
    Dr Sarah Maskell
Margaret & John Mason OAM
Don & Sue Matthews
Sandra Murdoch
Jane & Andrew Murray
Nelson Bros Funeral Services
The Orloff Family Charitable Trust

Jeremy Ruskin & Roz Zalewski
Brian Snape AM &
    Christina Martin
Geoff Steinicke
James & Anne Syme
Liz Tromans
The Veith Foundation
Price & Christine Williams
The Ray & Margaret Wilson
    Foundation
Gillian & Tony Wood
Anonymous (2)

LOYALTY CIRCLE

$1,000+

Prof Noel Alpins AM & Sylvia Alpins
Margaret Astbury
Ian Baker & Cheryl Saunders
Prof Robin Batterham
Sandra Beanham
Angelina Beninati
Judy Bourke
Steve & Terry Bracks AM
David Reckenberg & Dale Bradbury
Jenny & Lucinda Brash
Bernadette Broberg
Beth Brown &
    The Late Tom Bruce AM
Jannie Brown
Rob & Sal Bruce
Julie Burke
Katie Burke
Geoffrey Bush-Coote &
    Michael Riordan
Pam Caldwell
Helen & Dugald Campbell
John & Jan Campbell
Jessica Canning
Clare Carlson
Jenny & Stephen Charles AO
Chernov Family
Assoc Prof Lyn Clearihan &
    Dr Anthony Palmer
Susan Cohen
Sandy & Yvonne Constantine
Barry & Deborah Conyngham
Karen Cusack
Sue & John Denmead
Mark Duckworth PSM &
    Lauren Mosso
Dr Sally Duguid & Dr David Tingay
Pam Durrant
Bev & Geoff Edwards
Karen & David Elias
Nita Eng
Anne Evans & Graham Evans AO

Marian Evans
Dr Alastair Fearn
Peter Fearnside & Roxane Hislop
Paul & Mary Fildes
Grant Fisher & Helen Bird
Jan & Rob Flew
Rosemary Forbes & Ian Hocking
Bruce Freeman
Gaye & John Gaylard
Howard & Glennys Hocking
Fiona Griffiths & Tony Osmond
Gill Family Foundation
Ian & Wendy Haines
Charles Harkin
M D Harper
Mark & Jennifer Hayes
Luke Heagerty
Lorraine Hendrata
Brett & Kerri Hereward
Dr Alice Hill & Mark Nicholson
Emeritus Prof Andrea Hull AO
Nanette Hunter
Ann & Tony Hyams AM
Peter Jaffe & Judy Gold
Neil Jens
Colin & Helen Masters
Paula McKinnon & Troy Sussman
Ben Johnson & Mark McNamara
Sally & Rod Johnstone
Lesley & Ian Jones
Leah Kaplan & Barry Levy
Irene Kearsey & Michael Ridley
Malcolm Kemp
Daniel Kilby
Michael Kingston
Fiona Kirwan-Hamilton &
    Brett Parkin
Doris & Steve Klein
Marianne & Arthur Klepfisz
Larry Kornhauser & Natalya Gill
Dr Emma Jane Ladakis

Verona Lea
Alison Leslie
Xue Snowe Li
Peter & Judy Loney
Lord Family
Lording Family Foundation
Kerryn Lowe & Raphael Arndt
Ken & Jan Mackinnon
Karin MacNab
Natasha & Laurence Mandie
Chris Maple
Ian & Judi Marshman
Lesley Mason
Penelope McEniry
Heather & Simon McKeon
Garry McLean
Libby McMeekin
Emeritus Prof Peter McPhee AM
Rosemary Meagher &
    The Late Douglas Meagher
Fiona Menzies
Robert & Helena Mestrovic
Ann Miller AM
Ross & Judy Milne-Pott
MK Hope
Barbara & David Mushin
Dr Rosemary Nixon AM
Sarah Nguyen
Nick Nichola & Ingrid Moyle
Michele Nielsen
Dr Paul Nisselle AM & Sue Nisselle
Sally Noonan
David & Lisa Oertle
Dr Jane & Alan Oppenheim
In loving memory of Richard Park
Bruce Parncutt AO
Dr Annamarie Perlesz
Dare & Andrea Power
Peter Philpott & Robert Ratcliffe
D Probert
Philip & Gayle Raftery

Sally Redlich
Victoria Redwood
John & Veronica Rickard
Phillip Riggio
Ken & Gail Roche
Roslyn & Richard Rogers Family
S & S Rogerson
B & J Rollason
Sue Rose
Nick & Rowena Rudge
Jenny Russo
Edwina Sahhar
Margaret Sahhar AM
Sandi Foundation
    dedicated to Alec
Alex & Brady Scanlon Giving Fund
Sally & Tim Scott

FE Scott
Susan Selwyn & Barry Novy
Jacky & Rupert Sherwood
Diane Silk
Dr John Sime
Pauline & Tony Simioni
Jan Simon
Jane Simon & Peter Cox
Tim & Angela Smith
Annette Smorgon
Dr Ross & Helen Stillwell
Rosemary Stipanov
Shannon Super
The Stobart Strauss Foundation
Irene & John Sutton
Rodney & Aviva Taft
Charles Tegner

Frank & Mirium Tisher
John & Anna van Weel
Graham Wademan &
    Michael Bowden
Walter & Gertie Wagner
Kevin & Elizabeth Walsh
Pinky Watson
Kaye & John de Wijn
Ann & Alan Wilkinson
Robert & Diana Wilson
Ralph Wollner &
    The Hon Kirsty Macmillan SC
Mandy & Edward Yencken
Anonymous (27)

EDUCATION GIVING CIRCLE

Acknowledging supporters who are transforming the lives of young Victorians through theatre.

Alan & Mary-Louise
    Archibald Foundation
Joanna Baevski
Judy Bourke
Deborah Conyngham
Geoff Cosgriff
Ann Darby
Linda Herd
Larry Kornhauser OAM &
    Natalya Gill

Greig Gaily & Dr Geraldine Lazarus
Heather & Simon McKeon
The Myer Foundation
Tom & Ruth O'Dea
The Ian Potter Foundation
Christopher Reed
John & Veronica Rickard
Anne & Mark Robertson OAM
Ken & Gail Roche
Roslyn & Richard Rogers Family

Andrew Sisson AO &
    Tracey Sisson
Rob Stewart & Lisa Dowd
The Stirling Family
Ronella Stuart
Ann & Alan Wilkinson
The John & Myriam
    Wylie Foundation
Anonymous (8)

LEGACY CIRCLE

Acknowledging supporters who have made the visionary gesture of including
a gift to Melbourne Theatre Company in their will.

John & Lorraine Bates
Mark & Tamara Boldiston
Bernadette Broberg
Adam & Donna Cusack-Muller
Anne Evans & Graham Evans AO
Bruce Freeman
Peter & Betty Game
Edith Gordon

Fiona Griffiths
Linda Herd
Tony Hillery & Warwick Eddington
Jane Kunstler
Irene Kearsey
Robyn & Maurice Lichter
Dr Andrew McAliece &
    Dr Richard Simmie

Libby McMeekin
Peter Philpott & Robert Ratcliffe
Marcus Pettinato
Jillian Smith
Diane Tweeddale
Francis Vergona
Anonymous (14)

Thank you

Melbourne Theatre Company would like to thank the following organisations for their generous support.

Major Partner

Future Directors Initiative Partner

MinterEllison.

Major Marketing Partner

The Monthly
The Saturday Paper
7am

Associate Partners

Challis & Company
Tomorrow's leaders today

Frontier software
Human Capital Management
& Payroll Software/Services

K&L GATES

THE LANGHAM
MELBOURNE

Supporting Partners

COMMUNE
WINE

Genovese

invicium

THE LUXURY NETWORK®

METROPOLIS
EVENTS

QUEST
SOUTHBANK

southgate

Wilson Parking

Marketing Partners

CINEMA NOVA

RRR

Southbank Theatre Partners

mgc
THE MELBOURNE GIN COMPANY

SCOTCHMANS HILL
BELLARINE PENINSULA
VICTORIA
ESTABLISHED 1982

Business Collective Members

Committee for Melbourne

Leadership Collective Australia

Schuler Shook

Current as of April 2025.

www.ingramcontent.com/pod-product-compliance
Lightning Source LLC
Chambersburg PA
CBHW050023090426
42734CB00021B/3387